Catharine Robb Whyte, *Yoho Peak*
c.1935, oil on canvas, 22.6 × 28.3 cm., WyC.01.201

ISBN
0·920608·31·0 paperback
0·920608·32·9 hardcover

Colophon
Design: Edward Cavell
Typography: Paperwords, Calgary
Typeface: Garamond Book, Flange Light
Paper: Quintessence Dull
Separations: Colour Four, Calgary
Printing: Paperworks Press Limited, Calgary
Photography: Craig Richards, Ian Laing

Exhibition presented
June 1 - July 14, 1988

WHYTE MUSEUM OF THE CANADIAN ROCKIES
111 Bear Street • Box 160 • Banff • Alberta • T0L 0C0 • (403) 762-2291

MOUNTAIN GLORY

THE ART OF PETER AND CATHARINE WHYTE

Curator	Edward Cavell
Text	Jon Whyte

4

Peter Whyte, *Lake O'Hara and Mount Biddle*
1936, oil on canvas, 92.0 × 102.0 cm., WyP.02.36

Peter Whyte, *Peaks 3 and 4, Moraine Lake*
c.1950, oil on canvas, 25.3 × 30.3 cm., WyP01.423

FOREWORD

It is often said that someone closely involved with a particular subject "can't see the forest for the trees." Perhaps this has been the case with the Whyte Museum and the exhibition and publication of "Mountain Glory: The Art of Peter and Catharine Whyte."

Over the years those involved with the museum have produced a great volume of catalogues and books dealing with artists and exhibitions that have found their inspiration or subject matter in the Canadian Rockies. Yet during this time there has never been a major retrospective exhibition or an easily accessible publication on the work of the museum's founders, Peter and Catharine Whyte. (The museum did produce a limited edition commemorative portfolio and book, however). The occasion of the twentieth anniversary of the opening of the main museum building has acted as a catalyst to rectify this situation.

Heritage Collection curator Jon Whyte has produced an insightful and colourful text which describes the lives of his aunt and uncle, the influences at work on their paintings and the legacy in art and museum-making they have left to us. As well, we have incorporated plates of some of the Whytes' best works and have provided a number of black-and-white photographs from their personal archives.

We hope that you will find the exhibition and this publication worth the wait.

E.J. Hart
Director

DEDICATION

My friend Jon introduced me to his aunt Catharine Whyte in the late sixties. I was invited over for tea. In retrospect it was an initiation. When we arrived Catharine was mending something – socks I think – surrounded by tilting stacks of waiting to be read (and filed) *Calgary Heralds*. She was gracious, a little shy and seemingly interested in everything this naïve young fellow, fresh from the east, had to say. She made me a friend. Subsequent visits, occasionally extended by impromptu lunches of broiled cheese and bacon sandwiches, made me a fan.

Catharine's house was a delightful experience. Any opportunity to visit was a treat. It was floor to ceiling art, wall to wall life. Her days seemed over-full with interests and commitments, yet she responded with infinite patience to the endless interruptions caused by a stream of callers (somedays, someone every twenty minutes, from breakfast until well after dinner). Over time I began to realize how significant a contribution Catharine made to the community. Never mentioned by her, but quietly acknowledged by her friends, the measure of Catharine's generosity was considerable: support for Banff's returning soldiers, the Banff Centre's Margaret Greenham Theatre, the town's Recreation Centre, native schools, medical research, musicians, artists and just plain folk! The main recipient of her generosity was, of course, the museum she and Peter created in a demonstration of their limitless faith in the importance of civilization in the midst of this overwhelming wilderness.

The Whyte Museum is very much a reflection of Catharine. Peter is represented in his paintings and throughout the collections, but his death two years before the completion of the building somewhat neutralized his voice. The museum is permeated with Catharine's unique blend of energy, commitment and comfortable elegance. She is a continuing presence for the museum staff as we second guess what Catharine's position, on any topic, would have been. (It's amazing how selective the memory can be when trying to win a point. We all feel that Catharine would support our particular proposal!)

This exhibition and publication have been a labour of love for all of us at the museum. It's a genuine pleasure to give back a little after receiving so much. As Gus Benedetti, our Head of Maintenance Emeritus, pointed out to all new museum staff, the table lamp in the Swiss Guides Room is *always* left on "for Catharine."

Edward Cavell
Curator of Art

8

Catharine Robb Whyte, *Mount Temple, Larches*
c.1940, oil on canvas, 27.7 × 35.2 cm., WyC.01.412

Catharine Robb Whyte, *Bow Lake, Crowfoot Glacier*
c.1950, oil on canvas, 25.0 × 30.5 cm., WyC.01.313

MOUNTAIN LIVES

"As Pete says, we are just a couple of crazy artists, and now we realize it more than ever," Catharine Whyte wrote her mother at the end of 1933. "You feel it's useless to try to paint, for you just can't do what you want to with it; but you know you can't leave it and stop."[1]

Pete may have thought they were crazy, but crazy they were not. Methodical, conservative, and orthodox, always curious, would better describe their artistic attitudes and practices.

The Whytes met in 1925 at the School of the Museum of Fine Arts in Boston. Peter, his schooling complete in 1929, worked that summer at Lake Louise, made an outfitted trip to the Saskatchewan Glacier in the early fall with Gardner Cox (a fellow portraitist he had met at school), then worked his way around the world, sketching in Hawaii, Japan and China, while Catharine finished her education. They were wed at the end of June 1930. Over the winter of 1930-31 their summer studio-home in Banff was built while they helped run the Skoki Ski Camp, north-east of Lake Louise, started by Pete's brother Cliff and his boyhood chum Cyril Paris. In the winter-springs of '32 and '33 they managed Skoki. In April 1933 the avalanche death on Fossil Mountain of R.E.A.C. "Kit" Paley, a twenty-seven year old British mathematician who had been working with Norbert Wiener at MIT, ended their business involvement in skiing. They took the opportunity to paint and globe-trot.

Pete was born in Banff in January 1905. His New Brunswick-born father, Dave White,[2] a general merchant in the village, had been a CPR section man at Sawback west of Banff from 1886 until 1893. His Scottish-born mother, Annie, daughter of John Donaldson Curren, a coal scout and naïve painter, was raised in Anthracite, east of Banff. Pete benefited from the region's recreational opportunities: snowshoe outings, skiing, ski jumping, hiking and horseback riding. He was influenced to become an artist by the painters who lived in Banff: Belmore Browne (1880-1954, a remarkable outdoorsman-painter), Carl Rungius (1869-1959; North America's greatest game animal painter), and Nora Drummond-Davis (1862-1949, an illustrator for Raphael Tuck, a British

▲

Peter Whyte, 1927

1. Catharine Whyte, letter to her mother, Edith Robb, Dec. 29 1933. Catharine wrote swiftly and chattily, and rarely read her letters over to correct their spelling or punctuation. I have sometimes added punctuation to clarify her meaning.

2. Dave spelled his name "Whyte" until 1893-4 when he founded the Park Store in Banff. Family folklore says he changed it to "White" when a sign-painter up from Calgary spelled it that way; it was less bother – more frugal? – to change his name than to get the sign-painter back up. In 1927 Dorothy Whyte, a family friend (note her spelling) persuaded Pete the "y" held more cachet for an artist. My father Dave – called Jack – changed to the "y" until he became the manager-proprietor of Dave White & Sons in the early '30s. *JW*

postcard company). In his teens Pete took school courses in art given by Browne and Drummond-Davis, private lessons from Browne, and a correspondence course in cartooning.

In the tourist seasons of the 1920s Pete drove busses and limousines for the Brewster Transport Company, frequently chauffeuring movie stars like Anna May Wong, who played in *The Alaskan*, and Lillian Rich, whom he taught to ski. Because of his California friendships, he enrolled at the Otis

Catharine Robb Whyte, c.1922

Art School in Los Angeles in 1924-25. Pete met the New England landscape artist, Aldro T. Hibbard (1886-1972) in Banff and painted with him at Lake O'Hara in August 1925. Mr Hibbard persuaded him to enroll in Boston. There Pete met Catharine Robb, a half-day student that session who was seeing if she wished to pursue art as a career. They fell in love in 1927.

Catharine, born in June 1906, in Concord, Massachusetts, was an heir to New England's intellectual-artistic-business traditions. Edward Sylvester Morse, her maternal grandfather, a marine biologist and noted collector of Japanese ceramics, had been the first director of the Peabody Museum in Salem, Massachusetts. Her mother, Edith Morse Robb (1864-1962), a pioneer businesswoman in the 1890s, had designed and produced needlepoint patterns, and her Iowa-born father Russell Robb (1864-1927) was senior vice-president and treasurer of Stone & Webster, a major Boston engineering firm.

After private school in Providence, Rhode Island, Catharine made her bow to Boston society in 1924 – she did it to please her brother Russell, she said – then attended the Museum School from September 1925 to April 1930.

The Whytes' formal art training was academic: drawing from plaster casts for the first year, emphasizing materials and composition, then studying anatomy and drawing nudes and finally painting portraits in oil. Peter learned his landscape techniques from Browne, Hibbard, Rungius, and from J.E.H. MacDonald (1873-1933), the Toronto painter and oldest member of the Group of Seven who spent a month at Lake O'Hara, Yoho National Park, each summer from 1924 to 1930. Pete accompanied him at the invitation of the manager of Lake O'Hara Lodge,

Peter Whyte, *Bow Lake from the Summit*
c.1945, oil on canvas, 63.5 × 76.5 cm., WyP.02.15

Peter Whyte, *Mount Athabasca*
c.1945, oil on canvas, 27.7 × 35.4 cm., WyP.01.146

Sylvia "Sid" Brewster, who recognized Mr Mac-Donald's fear of the parks' wild animals. (In 1924 a cougar had followed him down the trail when he returned from sketching Lake Oesa.) In turn Catharine learned landscape technique from Pete.

In the 1930s the Whytes painted numerous portraits, choosing people with strong faces and historic importance, people like Tom Wilson and the chiefs of the Stoney Indians from the Morley Reserve, some sixty kilometres east of Banff. The Stoneys developed enduring friendships with Pete's father Dave when he was a bachelor section man west of Banff. The Indians, who forded the Bow River near his section house on their hunting trips to the Kootenay country on the far side of the Great Divide, stopped in for tea both coming and going, a social interlude for a man who had few visitors. Thereafter the Stoneys were always welcome in Dave White's home, and Pete admired their traditions, arts and crafts, liked their stories, and honoured their friendship, as Catharine would too.

Spring, summer, and autumn, forty to fifty days each year of the 1930s, except for 1934 when they were travelling and sketching in Japan, China and Bali, the Whytes were outdoors, painting strong, swift, small sketches of the mountain landscapes they loved. Sketched at their easels within calling distance of each other, in like weather and atmosphere, their field works strongly resemble each other's.[3] Carl Rungius "always said one never should sell one's samples, which he calls one's small sketches,"[4] so the Whytes rarely sold them. After the Whytes' deaths the Whyte Museum of the Canadian Rockies became the repository of those often bright, quick works. Weak 1930s art markets—nonexistent in prairie Canada—and the Whytes'

travel, photography, and skiing limited their output of large canvasses.

After a winter of skiing and sketching in Switzerland and painting in Norway in the spring of 1938, the Whytes returned to North America when the clouds of war in Europe became dense. That September in Banff Pete joked, "What with the threat of war in Europe, a hurricane in New England, and continued good weather here, I don't know what the world's coming to!"[5]

Recognizing both that world tensions would curtail their travels, obliging them to winter in

Peter and Catharine Whyte with an unidentified friend on the Lake O'Hara Road, c.1935

3. After Pete died in 1966, Catharine and I occasionally looked through the sketches stored in their studio. Some of Pete's uninventoried sketches had become intermingled in her stack. She genuinely could not say which of them had painted some of the numerous small unsigned works. People who express a preference for the works by either one of the Whytes should recall Catharine's confusions about some of their authorship.

4. Catharine Whyte, letter to her mother, Edith Robb, Jan. 12 1934.

5. Catharine Whyte, letter to her mother, Edith Robb, Sept. 27 1938.

Banff, and a need to extend their summer studio-home to accommodate their growing interests, the Whytes planned a wing for a carpentry shop, darkroom, a furnace to winterize their log home, and a second storey painting studio. When they had designed the house (it was mostly Pete's plan, based on Belmore Browne's Banff home), a studio next to the living room seemed easy to live with, but it created problems: visitors sometimes interrupted the artists in mid-portrait or commented on paintings in progress; and as the spruce around the Whytes' home grew, the light became inadequate. The wing, added to the home in October 1939, had one unforeseen consequence: Catharine never completed another studio-size painting. She stayed downstairs attending to business, correspondence, and housekeeping while Pete painted in the new studio. People unfamiliar with the richness, variety and depth of Catharine's correspondence may not understand how much she invested her artistic expression in her letters.[6]

The outbreak of the war kept the Whytes in Banff. Pete joined the Reserve Army in 1942, then enlisted in the Royal Canadian Air Force in March 1943. Posted to a "bush station" at Tofino, Vancouver Island, in August–where Catharine joined him in September–he entered and placed second in a servicemen's art competition in April 1944. Appointed to the Canadian War Art Programme at the end of May, he sketched aspects of the Commonwealth Air Training Programme on the Alberta prairies. As late as October he hoped to be posted overseas, but, Catharine wrote, "the Air Force is cutting down in every way they can and just don't want to give any more commissions out and also they aren't very keen anyway on giving them to artists. . . . It was quite a disappointment

all round, being keyed up to the thing, but Pete is very philosophical about it. . . . Well, if they don't want to use him that way, it's their loss, and we can look forward to painting together again all the sooner "[7]

Anxiety and alcoholism curtailed Pete's output after the war, but in April 1948 nineteen Rocky Mountain sketches by Peter and sixteen by Catharine were shown in London and Windsor, Ontario, an exhibit arranged by Clair Bice of the London gallery. The same selection was also shown in Concord in June, then in Tilsonburg, Kitchener, and Brantford, Ontario in early 1949; and their painter friends George Pepper (1903-1962) and Kathleen Daly Pepper (1898-) arranged an exhibit at Hart House and the Wakunda Art Centre at the University of Toronto in March.

Pete was unfailingly generous with his nieces and nephews–of which I was one–in the neighbourhood. He always had time for us, planning picnics, encouraging us in our skiing, attaching our ski bindings, or, for example, writing verse with me and amusing us with his deft cartoons. The Whytes extended that affection to all our friends. One incident will show his humour, affection, craftsmanship, and care. A dachshund pup came into our household about 1949; Pretzel that Christmas received a small bentwood mono-ski with a Huitfeldt binding Pete had made for him–to hold the elongated pup's stomach off the snow.

In 1952 Pete developed cataracts. After a first cataract operation in September 1953 he painted vigorously while he awaited the second cataract's maturation and a subsequent operation. During the period he finished eleven large works commissioned by Eric Harvie, the art patron,

---

6. Catharine wrote with grace, telling anecdotes swiftly and surely, capturing a personality and her emotions and attitudes. Always anxious about her writing, she never knew how well she wrote. Here's an anecdote about me, for example: "We often test people out for the fun on whether or not they notice the pictures. It is very interesting, for some see the pictures before noticing anything else in the house. Little Jonny" [I would be six in a day] "came over the other evening and right away noticed that we had an Indian head instead of the camp over the table, and then he remarked on the new pictures Pete had stacked on the floor. He often stands them where he can look at them to figure out what to do next. Jonny will sit on his heels and study them for a minute and then look up at me and say, 'They are pretty good, aren't they Catharine?' in the most professional manner." [Catharine Whyte, letter to her mother, Edith Robb, March 14 1947.] *JW*

7. Catharine Whyte, letter to her mother, Oct. 30 1944.

Catharine Robb Whyte, *Castle Mountain*
c.1950, oil on canvas, 25.4 × 30.3 cm., WyC.01.91

Catharine Robb Whyte, *Lake O'Hara from Opabin*
1931, oil on canvas, 22.2 × 27.7 cm., WyC.01.54

Peter and Catharine Whyte, c.1935

collector and founder of the Glenbow Museum, for the Luxton Museum in Banff, and several other large canvasses. Catharine increasingly dedicated her time to recording and collecting historical material and correspondence, spadework for what would become the Archives of the Whyte Museum of the Canadian Rockies. After Pete's recovery from cataracts he spent considerable time encouraging Walter J. Phillips (1884-1963), the Banff watercolourist who became afflicted with cataracts himself.

The Whytes continued sketching out-of-doors, but their output languished in the '60s. Pete's death in December 1966 hastened one major project. In June 1968 Catharine brimmed with joy as old-timer guide, neighbour and amateur watercolourist Jimmy Simpson (1877-1972) and cowboy sculptor Charlie Beil (1894-1976) cut a buckskin thong to open the building which has become the centre of the Whyte Museum.

That July Catharine joined Kathleen Daly Pepper for a sketching trip to Povungnituk, a northern Québec Inuit settlement, returning to portraiture after thirty years, her last flourish in painting. That summer and the next she painted several bright landscapes at Lake O'Hara, but, aside from a few half-hearted attempts at portraiture, she never again found time to paint.

Catharine once expressed her gratitude for the three different lives she had lived: the intense, socially ordered life in Concord and Boston; the quiet, essentially straightforward life of her marriage to Pete, and the worldly citizen she became after his death.

Community concerns, a return to skiing, travel, conservation activities, her concern and attention to the developing cultural institution she had launched next door, and her extensive philanthropy kept her constantly and intensely involved until her death in March 1979.

Peter Whyte, *Mount Assiniboine, September Snow*
c.1940, oil on canvas, 64.0 × 76.0 cm., WyP.02.09

Peter Whyte, *Skiing*
1938, oil on canvas, 27.8 × 35.2 cm., WyP.01.482

MOUNTAIN PAINTERS

Atop Tunnel Mountain above Banff, whither she had walked to be fit for a hiking excursion in Nepal in 1970, Catharine pointed out some striae, deep scratches in the limestone made by boulders borne along by the Bow Valley glacier some fifteen thousand years earlier. She told me that such scores serve for a compass in New England where glaciers had coursed north-south on their run to the Atlantic Ocean.

Did Catharine learn the observation from her mother, who learned it from her father, Edward Morse? It's a direct line. Mr Morse studied marine biology in the 1850s with Louis Agassiz, the father of palæontology and glaciology. Agassiz, who had formed his theories of glacial movement and continental glaciation in 1837, observed similar striae when he stepped off a boat from Europe and ascended the hills of Halifax in 1846. Peter and Catharine Whyte brought to their painting a learned awareness of how glaciers formed and are shaping the Rockies.

The Whytes adapted and reshaped the insights of their precursors, the English and Northern European painters whose traditions and techniques created a milieu for Canadian Rockies landscape painting, and the Canadian and American painters who painted the Rockies well in the fifty years from the early 1880s to the 1930s.

In the nineteenth century a belief in Nature's order, supported by geological awareness, created a secular faith centred on mountains, "the beginning and end of all natural scenery,"[8] as John Ruskin called them. The Rockies' first painters drew on the wellsprings of that world picture,

seeing nature anew in an age of adventure and discovery. By forging an awareness of deep time and stratigraphy–perceived by the Scottish father of geology, James Hutton–to unleashed Romanticism, Joseph M.W. Turner (1775-1851) made himself Europe's first fine mountain painter. As the newness of the Victorians' furied developments of geology, biology, evolution, and limnology have faded, mountain painting has become increasingly sentimentalized. Those mountain painters who are ignorant of geology fail to understand how what they see was shaped, and feel landscape inadequately.

Mountain life includes risk, threat, and danger, the marginality and delicacy of alpine life, exposure, extremes of weather, and loneliness. Good mountain painting explores those themes, and develops them in contrasting ways. In *Modern Painters* John Ruskin, the poet of the alpine, distinguishes mountain gloom from mountain glory, contrasting the desperate lives of mountain dwellers with the grandeur of their landscape. The viewer of mountain pictures can spend intriguing hours testing how artists counterpoint those alpine extremes. To point the way: mountain gloom creeps into Pete's sketches, the glory in Catharine's. Yet in Pete's gloomiest works, ecstatic possibility gleams forth; in Catharine's most glorious moments, the gloom is in the shadow. As Ruskin says, "no good or lovely thing exists in this world without its correspondent darkness."[9]

The Rockies were revealed for the first time in an age of adventure by the painters who influenced the Whytes. Carl Rungius spent more years exploring mountain and alpine wilderness than any other painter: five summers in Wyoming's Wind River Range, and a summer in the Yukon

---

8. John Ruskin, *Modern Painters*, Vol. IV, (Part V, "Of Mountain Beauty"), 1888, p. 353.

9. *Ibid.*, p. 351.

mountains before he began his forty-five summers and autumns in the Canadian Rockies in 1910. Belmore Browne virtually reached the summit of Mt McKinley in 1912,[10] six years before he moved to Banff. Aldro Hibbard knew Vermont's glaciated mountains and understood the shifting light on snow as few other painters have. Their love for the high, bright landscape hardened the art of both J.E.H. MacDonald, who brought his educated eye for composition to them, and Lawren Harris (1885-1970), his fellow in the Group of Seven, the only successful Rocky Mountain abstractionist. All these painters, except Lawren Harris, influenced the Whytes' mountain painting. (When Pete and Catharine saw Harris' mountain work in February 1931, Catharine said, "He changes things from literal to the opposite in order to give you the feeling of the place, which he does succeed in doing. It was very interesting seeing what he did with places we are familiar with in the mountains."[11] But she also recalled their embarrassment at not knowing what to say when they saw the works. Harris' mountains, they thought, looked like they had been formed in jelly moulds.[12])

Raised in Concord, Massachusetts, the United States' most fertile ground for the literary-*cum*-natural history awareness, Catharine respected its Ralph Waldo Emerson-Henry David Thoreau tradition, but never read *Walden* nor *A Week on the Concord and Merrimack Rivers*, and voiced the town's belief that Thoreau was a wastrel, having let his father's pencil factory languish. She was intrigued by J.E.H. MacDonald's having named his son Thoreau in honour of the Concord philosopher. She ardently supported the preservation of wilderness, and Pete's works and hers are hymns to wildness, but Thoreau's ideas came to her indirectly.

23

From the Turner tradition the Whytes' routes diverge, as I have suggested. In Pete's paintings, gloomy, tragic, foreboding, hostile peaks hover over shadowed slopes. He responds to mountains with emotions something like a climber's, ambiguously loving and fearing them. Catharine loves sky and weather's brief moments. Since light and shadow intrigue her, she pursues effect more than form. Peter's compositional rigor – MacDonald's lesson – is so firm we seek to no avail the light which creates such strong relief, whereas we have no doubt what light rakes Catharine's scenes. Natural forces animate her sketches: sunlight, wind, storm, the dazzle of sunlight on water, the changing of seasons,

Catharine Whyte, Adeline Link, J.E.H. MacDonald and Peter Whyte on the Opabin Moors, Lake O'Hara, 1930

10. Belmore Browne, *The Conquest of Mount McKinley*, New York: G.P. Putnam's Sons, the Knickerbocker Press, 1913.

11. Catharine Whyte, letter to her mother, Feb 24 1931.

12. Personal reminiscence, *JW*

Peter Whyte, *Lake O'Hara*
1935, oil on canvas, 63.5 × 76.2 cm., WyP.02.39

the flame of aspens in autumn. Pete, in his studio paintings more than in his sketches, loves working in the dark, shadowed zones of a picture, working dark against dark in a barely discernible richness.

Catharine did not believe herself that the painting of others influenced their work. Pointing out a foreground tree in one of Pete's paintings one day (page 24), I asked Catharine how familiar they were with Group of Seven paintings in 1935. She listed MacDonald, Harris, Lismer, adding that they met A.Y. Jackson and saw his works later; then asked why I wanted to know. "It looks like a 'Group of Seven tree,'" I said. She said it was a real tree, that they painted what they saw: "We didn't make things up or borrow them." Some months later, when Catharine and I were at Lake O'Hara, I suggested we go seek the tree. We couldn't find it. "It must have fallen down," she said.

Nuance of emotion enriches both their works. Dread is absent from Pete's Stoney tepee camps, town-scapes, and winter paintings, but the guise of humor, black or mellow, in his "people-scapes" (the ski cartoons, *The Funeral of David Bearspaw* [page 27], the Indian camp paintings) reveals a subtle anxiety. Sometimes, as in the "Funeral," he even creates a kind of paradoxical joy in a sad occasion, an opposition to his ironic dread-laden alpine meadows.

When I read the diaries Catharine wrote when she was a teenager, I understood, as I had not before, that her sketches' often stormy skies embody her strong emotions. People may read her landscapes as simple depiction, but this always dynamic, congenial, considerate, charitable, and democratic woman, her face illuminated by a smile and her love of life, created pic-

25

tures surprising to us who thought we knew her. The tension created by a serene foreground lake and a storm-threatened sky excites her; such themes are revealing self-portraits. She animates her skies in a way that Peter rarely does. To get more sky and light into a sketch, she places her horizons lower. Catharine knew, as Ruskin said, "there are effects by tens of thousands, for ever invisible and inconceivable to the inhabitant of the plains, manifested among the hills in the course of one day. The mere power of familiarity with the clouds, of walking with them and above them, alters and renders clear our whole conception of the baseless architecture of the sky;

▲

Peter Whyte sketching at Lake O'Hara, c.1930

Peter Whyte, *Mrs Tom Simeon*
1931, oil on canvas, 75.0 × 62.0 cm., WyP.02.25

Peter Whyte, *The Funeral of Chief David Bearspaw*
1956, oil on canvas, 90.5 × 100.8 cm., WyP.02.33

and for the beauty of it, there is more in a single wreath of early cloud, pacing its way up an avenue of pines, or pausing among the points of their fringes, than in all the white heaps that fill the arched sky of the plains from one horizon to the other."[13]

Neither Peter nor Catharine climbed mountains, though they crossed Abbot Pass from Lake O'Hara to Lake Louise (a photo taken that September 19 1930 is the source of the Museum's logo), reached the summit of Ptarmigan Peak near Skoki in April 1932, and explored the Drummond Glacier on skis. Ardent members of the Sky Line Trail Hikers of the Canadian Rockies, they loved hiking, and the larch-fringed alpine country exhilarated them both. On a three-day hiking and sketching trip from Moraine Lake to Lake O'Hara when the Whytes camped on the Opabin Dome, Catharine was thrilled when Pete gently awoke her to tell her a mouse which had built a nest in her hair was still asleep there.

One aspect of the Rockies is more apparent in the Whytes' sketches than it is in any other painters' works. The products of omnipresent icefields and relatively recent glaciation (the major glaciers of the range retreated above the alpine some twelve thousand years ago), more lakes and tarns dot the Rockies than any other of the world's mountain ranges. Casual viewers of the Rockies see the "naturally" picturesque aspects of the Whytes' sketches, misinterpreting the colour perceptions in their many Lake O'Hara and Bow Lake paintings as willful exaggeration.

Given Catharine's generosity of spirit and her love of people, it is surprising that, apart from her portraits of the 1930s and 1968, people occur so infrequently in her works. Pete is the painter of town-scapes, Stoney Indian camps, skiers, buildings, settlements. One explanation is that while Pete went out sketching the neighbourhood, Catharine attended to shopping, cooking, letter writing and business when the Whytes were in Banff. But she also envied Pete's skill in capturing something he learned from cartooning: the quick rendering of gesture which is the strength of caricature. She knew she capably captured character in a portrait—and more than once told me her 1931 portrait of the pioneer guide-outfitter Tom Wilson (page 30) "got the likeness" in a way that Pete's did not. But an artist who loved the texture of mountain form, a recorder of momentary phenomena, a colourist, she was more painter than draughtsman.

Though Catharine actively generated ideas and put them into action in museum building, conservation and the community, and though both Whytes had definite tastes in art, they said little about ideas in their own art. When they were reading Rockwell Kent's (1882-1971) essays and introductions in *Rockwellkentiana*[14] in 1933, Catharine got as close to expressing the anguish of painting as she ever would, writing, "I guess most people like that boy on Mt Monadnock think of artists that 'they just daub the paint on,' but it certainly means a lot of upsetting thought as well. . . . To most people artists lead such a pleasant sort of life and whenever they like they can go out and paint a 'pretty picture,' but after you get beyond that stage it's the most discouraging sort of work. . . . We've just begun to see what we are trying to do, and have decided that it's the thought behind the painting that makes the picture. It's wonderful to be able to discuss the whole thing together, but sometimes we get so worked up we can't sleep. . . . We know what we want to do and how we want to paint, but we're so far from being able to do it."[15]

13. Ruskin, *op. cit.*, p. 358.

14. Rockwell Kent, *Rockwellkentiana*, New York: Harcourt, Brace and Company, 1933.

15. Catharine Whyte, letter to her mother, Edith Robb, Dec. 29 1933.

How do I balance their achievements and their failures? Their *plein-air* "samples" are frequently as fine as MacDonald's, Rungius' and Browne's: brightly seen, vividly felt, unique contributions to the visual history of the Rockies. I feel no embarrassment in making the comparisons. Peter's relatively few big paintings are solidly built and often moving, though they lack the spark of the smaller works. His ski paintings are unequalled in Canadian art. Catharine's handsome portraits – and some of Pete's – capture personality and period with an awareness of the sitters' dignity and history. My regrets – and I am not alone – are that Catharine never made time to finish any large landscapes, that her large portraits number only three – one of them lost! – that Pete, an accomplished painter, took an easy route, spending months at a time in mediocre photography, and he lost his sense of challenge too early. I do not doubt the excellence of what they did produce; they rank with the best of their contemporaries in painting the Rockies. But their innate aesthetic conservatism reined them too tightly; they turned aside too early from what others, like Lawren Harris, were doing, and they did not challenge each other to achieve the greatness they could have attained. They were not dilletantes, but their generosity of spirit allowed others to distract them from one of their two potential contributions. They made their mountain community richer by creating a museum, but it is our loss that they did not leave the legacy of a growing aesthetic vision that seemed so attainable in the early 1930s.

Catharine Robb Whyte, *Tom Wilson*
1932, oil on canvas, 74.9 × 62.2 cm., WyC.02.05

Catharine Robb Whyte, *Chief Dan Wildman*
1930, oil on canvas, 76.7 × 63.4 cm., WyC.02.01

THE WHYTES' MUSEUM

Both the Whyte Museum of the Canadian Rockies, one of the world's smaller international museums, and New York's vast American Museum of Natural History have roots in Harvard's Museum of Comparative Zoölogy (known popularly as the Agassiz Museum). Albert S. Bickmore and Edward Sylvester Morse, students of the dynamic, mercurial, handsome, Swiss-born naturalist Louis Agassiz (1807-1873) at Harvard College, Cambridge, worked with him in his development of a teaching museum in 1860. A decade later Mr Bickmore enlisted the support of well-to-do New Yorkers to found the American Museum, and from 1866 to 1871 Mr Morse became a curator at the newly established Peabody Academy of Science in Salem, Massachusetts. He became its director from 1880 to 1914.

Mr Morse (1838-1925), an ebulliently broad American Victorian intellectual, was a marine biologist who wrote a first textbook on zoölogy. But he also concentrated his polymathic mind on topics as diverse as "The Suppression of Unnecessary Noise" and *Mars and its Mysteries* (with Percival Lowell), gathered an almost Linnæan collection of Japan's pottery, whither he had gone in 1877 to study its "great green brachiopods" and, when he discovered Jomon period potsherds in a five thousand year old shell midden at Omori near Tokyo, introduced archæology to the country. First Director of the Peabody Institute, a museum with biological, anthropological, marine and maritime collections, Morse influenced his granddaughter Catharine Robb Whyte in collecting, writing history, annotating objects and museum-making.

George K.K. Link

In the 1950s the Whytes, who had postponed raising a family until it was too late, began considering what to do with their combined inheritances of wealth and property. Long interested in the history and culture of the Rockies, they had been acquiring properties along the Bow River frontage beside their home, and began firming up ideas. Catharine, who at twelve said "drawing and reading" were her keenest interests, was anxious to provide Banff with a library; the development of the Luxton Museum in the town had diverted the Whytes' interest in developing a showplace for Stoney Indian costume and culture; and they regretted how few places artists could exhibit their works in western Canada.

▲

Catharine Whyte (top), Rudolph Aemmer, Peter Whyte and Neil Begg on the pinnacle at Abbot Pass, 1930

In May 1958 Catharine wrote her mother about their ideas for "an Art Gallery and Library or perhaps some sort of historical museum."[16] Later that month they sought the help of their friend George Maclean, Walking Buffalo, for "a name that wasn't too long, but suitable for a place where there were paintings and books and our ground[s] with the grass and trees."[17] The Stoney medicine man considered the problem, then said "Wa-Che-Yo-Cha-Pa," and tried to explain what it meant: "'Anything you see, anything you do, it's perfect. Doesn't matter what you do or what you see. All there. Would draw influence.' (by that he meant it would be educational) 'in that way perfect, in that way nice and beautiful. Your mind draws to the work, and the influence draws. Can't say nothing against.'"[18] Catharine and her journalist nephew David Stockand later pooled their talents to paraphrase Walking Buffalo's words as "where the good, the wise and the beautiful come together in harmony," the phrase which has guided the policies of the Whyte Museum of the Canadian Rockies.

Wa-Che-Yo-Cha-Pa became the name of the Foundation the Whytes created then. Its board of trustees renamed it the Peter Whyte Foundation in 1972, six years after Pete's death, and the Peter and Catharine Whyte Foundation in March 1979, after Catharine's death.

The Whytes' ideas about culture (Catharine loved the concept, hated the word) were broad, textured, and seamless. They did not separate their painting from their recreation, nor history from art, nor community from the life of the mind, nor beauty from the practical. In their home bright or interestingly shaped rocks are placed by fine Japanese pots, a Belmore Browne sketch hangs beside a Stoney Indian knife sheath,

33

a plain-Jane New England chair sits on a frayed but comfortable Persian carpet, a Mongolian crossbow rests on an eighteenth century English chest. A wedding gift from John D. Rockefeller III–a girlhood beau of Catharine's–an Oriental pottery lamp, for which she made a parchment and buckskin shade, lights some small, fine Inuit soapstone carvings, an Indian basket filled with Japanese fishing floats which Pete picked up on Vancouver Island and gave Catharine for Christmas 1943, and a Cambodian papier-maché box filled with flamingo feathers they picked up in the Caribbean in 1931.

In history and document collecting they saved everything: their own letters to each other, photographs of their families from well back into the nineteenth century, other photographs–mostly of the Rockies–that came into their hands, tape recordings they made of Stoney drumming and dancing, and an inordinate number of broadcasts of "Hawaii Calls," interviews with old (and not-so-old) timers, all their receipts, house plans

Whyte Museum of the Canadian Rockies

16. Catharine Whyte, letter to her mother, Edith Robb, May 15 1958.

17. Catharine Whyte, letter to her mother, Edith Robb, May 28 1958.

18. Ibid.

34

Catharine Robb Whyte, *Mount Biddle, Lake McArthur*
c.1935, oil on canvas, 27.6 × 35.2 cm., WyC.01.416

Catharine Robb Whyte, *Larch Trees*
c.1935, oil on canvas, 22.6 × 28.0 cm., WyC.01.350

and modifications, postcards, issues of *Life* and *The Beaver,* the bulletins of the Ski Club of Great Britain, and on and on and on.

The Whytes were not mere packrats, for Catharine had picked up her father's skill for organization. Were a caller to bring up an obscure fact about the Kicking Horse Tearoom, Catharine would scurry upstairs to return a minute later with the café's menu for 1936.

That assiduous, energetic collecting, which continued all their lives, became the groundwork for what in 1967 became the Archives of the Whyte Museum.[19] In 1987 an inventory of the contents of Catharine's own metres of personal papers and printed records in the Archives was prepared and circulated. For numerous reasons–including artistic, photographic, architectural, ethnological, skiing, and Rockies social history, among many others–it is a great Canadian collection of personal papers.

The Archives became a function of the Foundation in 1967. Maryalice Stewart, the first archivist, began to acquire papers, publications and documents from the community. Peter's illness in 1966 had sped up Catharine's planning, and she and Philippe Delesalle and Maryalice began planning a building for a more permanent home for the archives than the basement in which its collections had been temporarily stored, an art gallery, and a home for the Banff Library. In September 1967 Catharine turned the sod for the building, calling it her centennial project. It opened June 16 1968, dedicated to the "Banff pioneers," and exhibiting the first formal display of Pete's paintings and sketches in his home town. (The Banff School of Fine Arts had mounted a small selection of their sketches for a weekend in August 1949. Catharine sometimes

tutted the art school's failure to recognize the significance of Banff's painters: it never hired or called on Browne, Rungius, Beil, Nicholas de Grandmaison [1892-1978], Pete or herself.)

The building answered the Whytes' perception of a shortcoming in Banff: a gallery in which to display paintings, first called the Peter Whyte Gallery. But it was more than a space, for it was also a collection: Pete and Catharine's sketches and paintings, and the many other works of art the Whytes had collected before and during their marriage, are the basis of the 3,500 items it now contains.

In 1971 the Whytes' longtime friend Pearl Moore (1889-1973), a native Banffite, willed her home and the antique, art, taxidermic and Indian collections of her husband Philip (1879-1951) and herself to Catharine in trust to go to the museum. The Whytes had wanted the foundation to preserve their own home as "an example of a pleasant way of living in these times," but Pearl's bequest officially began the Heritage Collection, the museum's cultural history department.

The insight and foresight of its creators still guide the Whyte Museum of the Canadian Rockies. A small, dynamic museum, responsive to the internationally famous geography it celebrates and the community in which it is located, the Whyte Museum looks to the future, but its past directs it to and through the passes it must surmount. Peter and Catharine Whyte provided the parklike setting, started its collections, provided an initial endowment and gave its collections a home. However, it is for the present generation of mountain lovers to continue to ensure the richness of its collections and its ability to meet the physical and financial challenge of preserving the culture of the Canadian Rockies.

19. I have used few of the varied names of the Museum. The main building, when the Wa-Che-Yo-Cha-Pa Foundation opened it in 1967, contained the Archives of the Canadian Rockies, the Peter Whyte Gallery, and the Banff Library. The Foundation has renamed itself twice: the Peter Whyte Foundation in 1971; the Peter and Catharine Whyte Foundation in 1979. In 1983 the Foundation gave the property adjacent to the Museum to the Banff Library so it could have its own building, and developed a "Heritage Collection" gallery in the space the library had occupied. In 1985 the institution became the Whyte Museum of the Canadian Rockies, and simplified its department names to Archives, Galllery, and Heritage Collection. The Museum encompasses six buildings: the main Museum, the Whyte and Moore Homes, and three cabins. In addition the Museum provides a location for "Windy," an early Warden Cabin from the Cascade District which is owned by the Canadian Parks Service.